Thank you for your interest

If you would like more information about running Alpha for Prisons, please contact one of the following:

Alpha Canada
Box 153, 3456 Dunbar Street
Vancouver, B.C. V6S 2C2
Tel: 800-743-0899
Fax: 604-224-6124
Email: office@alphacanada.org
www.alphacanada.org

Alpha USA
74 Trinity Place
New York, NY 10006
Tel: 888-Why-Alpha
Fax: 212-406-7521
Email: info@alphausa.org
www.alphausa.org

In addition, there are Alpha Advisors who are experienced in prison ministry and would be happy to speak to you. To find your closest Prison Alpha Advisor, please check Alpha News or call the Alpha office for your country.

Alpha

Training Manual   Training Manual

Training Manual   Training Manual

Alpha for Prisons
Training Manual

Training Manual   Training Manual

Training Manual   Training Manual

Training Manual   Training Manual

Training Manual   Training Manual

Training Manual   Training Manual

Training Manual   Training Manual

Training Manual   Training Manual

Training Manual   Training Manual

THE A-Z OF HOW TO RUN ALPHA FOR PRISONS

Training Manual   Training Manual

Training Manual   Training Manual

Training Manual   Training Manual

North American edition contributing editors: Angela M. Burrin, Jeff T. Park, Ray Scanlan

Cover photo: © 2002 Getty Images; EyeWire

This edition published by Alpha Resources, Alpha North America, 74 Trinity Place, New York, NY 10006.

ISBN: 1-931808-562

1 2 3 4 5 6 7 8 9 10 Printing/Year 06 05 04 03 02

CONTENTS

FOREWORD

The growth of the Alpha course in prisons has been one of the most exciting developments in Christian missions for many years.

In 1996 there were eight prisons running the Alpha course in the United Kingdom. Now over 133 of the U.K.'s 160 prisons run Alpha.

The first Canadian Alpha for Prisons course was run in 1996. In 1998 the Alpha course was offered in the U.S. for the first time in a prison in Texas. Since then, courses have been run in over 40 states. The number of courses continues to expand, touching lives in prisons around the world.

This manual will help chaplains and prison workers make their Alpha course as effective as possible in the prison where they are working. It has been written from the experience gained by chaplains and course leaders in prisons in the U.K. and throughout North America.

Our prayer is first that through Alpha many more lives would be changed by God, secondly, that ex-offenders would be rehabilitated successfully back into society, and thirdly that re-offending rates would be reduced.

Nicky Gumbel

CHAPTER ONE

INTRODUCTION

This manual is designed to take you through the various stages of setting up and running an Alpha course in your local prison. The following pages aim both to equip and encourage you to present the Christian message in a way that is relevant to men and women in prison today.

All Alpha courses being run in prisons are slightly different and not all of the suggestions made in this manual will apply to your course, but the aim is to provide a framework to help you get started. Try to have a good look through this manual before you start planning your course and then use it for reference as you work through the course.

In this manual any reference to "prison" refers to any jail, detention center or other correctional facility.

WHAT IS ALPHA?

Alpha is a 15-session practical introduction to the Christian faith designed primarily for non-churchgoers and new Christians. The syllabus for the course is contained in the book *Questions of Life* by Nicky Gumbel. The Alpha course is a low key and nonthreatening series of sessions where men and women from any background or belief system can ask questions about the meaning of life.

Depending on the regime of each prison, sessions may be run in the morning, afternoon, or evening. If the session is not able to begin with a light snack or meal, we suggest a short time of fellowship before presenting the talk on a subject central to the Christian faith. Inmates on the course then break into pre-arranged groups (in which they remain for the entire course) to discuss the talk in an environment where each person should feel free to ask or express whatever they wish. There are three talks during which the subject of the Holy Spirit is addressed. If a full day cannot be set aside to present these talks, then they can be given at three consecutive sessions.

REALIZING THE NEED FOR ALPHA FOR PRISONS

- Currently in the U.S. there are more than two million men and women incarcerated in jails and prisons.
- In 2001 more than 109,000 young offenders were held in U.S. juvenile facilities.
- In 2001 there were 58,000 inmates in 219 Canadian prisons and jails. Of these inmates, 25,000 were young offenders, 12 to 17 years of age.

Alpha for Prisons was launched in the U.K. in December 1994 in response to demand from inmates with the desire to live changed lives. Prisons can be a place of hopelessness and depression. In the words of an ex-offender: *"Prisons are so final and leave you feeling hopeless. What is on offer through Alpha —is hope."*

WHO IS RUNNING ALPHA FOR PRISONS?

Alpha has been designed as a tool that any denomination or organization can feel comfortable using. Worldwide, courses have been run by chaplains of all denominations, a variety of organizations, and local churches. The potential of Alpha for Prisons is unlimited. Through the Alpha course prisoners are becoming Christians. Friendships are being built, inmates are supporting one another, and most importantly, incarcerated men and women are coming into a personal relationship with God through Jesus Christ.

WHO CAN RUN ALPHA IN A PRISON?

1. Prison chaplaincy
Prison chaplains have a challenging role. Chaplains may be responsible for several hundred men or women, most of whom are not Christians. Alpha for Prisons is being run by both single denomination and ecumenical chaplaincy teams around the world. Chaplains have access to facilities and play a vital role as liasons between prisoners, local church groups, and Christian organizations who want to run a course. Chaplains can help with the talks and also encourage and train the prisoners to lead the discussion groups in the second part of each session.

Some chaplaincies have adopted Alpha for Prisons as the principal means of evangelism in the prison. It is often new Christians who have just come to an Alpha course who encourage and cause others around them to come to the next course. New Christians can be fed into the existing structures of discipleship within the chaplaincy.

If you are a prison chaplain, try to involve any volunteers from local churches who are assisting you in your ministry, encouraging them to lead and help in small groups and to assist with other logistics, or to run the course themselves. If you do not have any volunteers, you will be able to locate churches running Alpha in your area from the Alpha register found in *Alpha News* or on the website (www.alphausa.org). It is often worth contacting the church to ask for their help in running the course in your prison.

2. Local church

Many local churches are positioned close to a prison and may have members of their congregation involved in the work of the prison. Some churches have provided speakers, leaders, and helpers for the Alpha course in their local prison. Local church support has proved invaluable when planning the Holy Spirit day and providing continuity for the follow up of new Christians. Prisoners value local church support and the partnership is vital. In the words of an inmate called Paul: "We need you—the church. We don't want to backslide. We don't want to be lost again. Many of us will feel nervous when we leave prison, not least because forgiveness is not a politically correct word. The fear of not being welcomed by our own Christian brothers and sisters is the worst fear of all."

It is essential that those running the course work closely within the regulations of the prison, so that they do not jeopardize the relationship with the prison authorities or put anyone at risk.

Make sure that you have consulted your prison chaplain or the relevant prison authority before you run Alpha. If you have never been into a prison, it may help to link with an experienced prison ministry team from another church or organization in your area and run the course together, as training is required.

3. Officers

In the U.K. a number of prison officers have run Alpha courses for inmates and for fellow colleagues in their prison. You may like to check with the chaplaincy to see if they are running or would like to run a course for officers.

4. Christian organizations

Various Christian organizations run Alpha for Prisons as part of their outreach. This enables them to feed new Christians into their existing structures of Bible studies and discipleship groups.

5. Inmates on the tiers/units

In our experience inmates have proven the best at reaching fellow inmates and inviting them to a course. In prisons where Alpha has been run for a number of years, prisoners are encourged to take responsibility for the advertising, planning, and running of courses. Such Alpha courses have proven to be very successful.

PLANNING YOUR COURSE—SEVEN STEPS TO A SUCCESSFUL COURSE

STEP #1: CONSULT YOUR CHAPLAINCY TEAM/CONTACT THE ALPHA U.S. OR ALPHA CANADA OFFICE, OR ONE OF THE PRISON ALPHA ADVISORS LISTED IN ALPHA NEWS.

Check with your chaplaincy team about whether they are already running an Alpha course and if not you may wish to consult them about starting one. Prison volunteers should schedule a time to meet with the chaplain, and bring a copy of the Alpha brochure, the Introduction to Alpha video, and some copies of *Alpha News*, to help describe and explain the course. Once the course is set, work out details such as meeting times (1 1/2–2 hours), food issues, Holy Spirit day and so forth.

The role of the advisors from the national offices in the U.S. and Canada is to support each Alpha course being run in a prison. We will attempt to answer any questions you may have about Alpha for Prisons, and also help get your course up and running, by providing the following:

- Alpha Resources are available by calling 1-800-36-ALPHA in the U.S. or 1-800-743-0899 in Canada. (See pages 14–15 for details.)
- Link to a prison running Alpha under similar circumstances—Many other courses are being run in all categories and types of prisons. It is often good to communicate with those running a course under similar conditions. You can also contact the Prison Alpha Advisor in your area (details in *Alpha News*).
- Advice on running the Holy Spirit day—Check with your Prison Alpha Advisor for ideas and advice.

Step #2: Attend an Alpha conference.

The two-day Alpha conferences are designed to train and equip you and your team to run an Alpha course. They cover the principles and the practicalities of the Alpha course and include a "Model Alpha Session." Nicky Gumbel has said that, "Running Alpha without attending a conference is like driving a car without taking any lessons."

For upcoming Alpha conferences, please see the latest edition of *Alpha News* or the Alpha website (www.alphausa.org in the U.S. or www.alphacanada.org in Canada). Prison seminars are offered at some of the Alpha conferences. Check with your U.S. or Canada Alpha Office or Prison Alpha Advisors for more information.

The aims of the Alpha conference are as follows:
(a) To explain the theological and practical reasons for running Alpha
(b) To provide all the practical training needed to run an effective Alpha course
(c) To model and explain the place of the following on an Alpha course through:

• Worship
• Talks (including a model Alpha evening)
• Prayer ministry
• Small group training

(d) To provide opportunities for prayer ministry

Step #3: Plan your team and appoint a course leader.

TEAM

It is vital to get the right people leading and helping with your Alpha course. The right team transforms a course and directly affects the number of guests attending Alpha. The ideal team to run Alpha in prison would be made up of volunteers who have already had experience in prison visiting and ministry. We suggest limiting table groups to eight inmates with no more than two outside leaders per table group. In prisons where the Alpha course is run regularly, inmates who have completed a course are encouraged, following training, to help lead small groups in future courses.

Leaders and helpers in Alpha should be positive, outgoing people who relate well to those outside the church. There is a simple test for good leaders and helpers. Ask yourself: "Would I happily put my closest friend who is not a Christian in that person's group?"

ALPHA COURSE LEADER

The course leader would benefit from having attended an Alpha conference and having done several Alpha courses. They will host each Alpha session, including the team training sessions, and will have pastoral responsibilities for the course. If the leader is not already on the chaplaincy team but is from a local church, it is helpful if he or she has had some experience with speaking in prison before being made the course leader.

STEP #4: TRAIN YOUR TEAM.

The team should be trained using the Alpha team training material, which is available from Alpha Resources (see pages 14–15 for more information). If the team members have no experience in prison work, it may be useful to invite a prison chaplain or worker to speak to your group about regulations, security, and the practicalities of ministering in a prison environment. Almost all prisons will require volunteers to go through an orientation on prison rules and regulations.

The following points should be covered:

PRAYER

- for personal and family protection
- unity of team
- access into the prison with associated security issues
- understanding the prison rules and regulations
- every aspect of the Alpha course
- for fruit

VISITORS INFORMATION SHEET (p.49)

- Work through this, highlighting some special points, i.e., numbers: 4, 5, 6, 8, 13, 14, 15, 16, 19, 20, 23, 26

SMALL GROUPS

Do not be shocked by points raised by inmates and look for future leaders and helpers.

HOLY SPIRIT DAY

During Holy Spirit day we have often found that inmates ask for prayer for members of their family. This may be a method of deflecting from the more challenging issue of prayer for themselves. Be prepared for this, and always suggest praying initially for the inmate.

BIBLES

Some churches donate Bibles, Alpha Course manuals, or the booklet *Why Jesus?* to each inmate at the beginning of Alpha. Members of the church congregation might like to write (in the front of the Bible) adding an appropriate verse to personalize the gift.

Remember the rule, "Nothing in—Nothing out." This also applies to Bibles and books, so permission from the authorities is required.

STEP #5: REGISTER YOUR ALPHA COURSE.

It's easy to register your prison's Alpha course:

1. In the U.S. call 1-800-36-ALPHA.
2. In Canada call 1-800-743-0899.

The Alpha U.S. and Canadian offices encourage all chaplaincies, churches and Christian organizations running Alpha for Prisons to register their courses. Not only is it encouraging to know the growth of the course in prisons in the U.S. and Canada, but such information allows us to network people for the sharing of experiences, support and help with the logistics of running Alpha in the prison environment.

It will also allow you to receive information about special events that may be taking place.

Step #6: Set the dates, deciding when you will hold the Holy Spirit day, and select a location.

Based on the anticipated size of the course, select a site for the weekly meetings.

Setting—As a general rule the more flexible the setting the better. The prison chapel is often the best place for privacy.

Small group space—If possible ensure that your location has enough space for the small groups to meet in private.

Bookings—Reserve all the rooms that will be needed for every aspect of the course so that there is no clash with other events.

Decide on the time needed for your course. Turn to page 20 for ideas on how to structure your course. Select a morning, afternoon, or evening carefully so as not to coincide with other Christian meetings or prison events. Plan time for the two team training sessions before the course starts. These are great opportunities to pray for those who will come to the course and to bond as a team.

Training session 3 looks at the subject of ministry, and should take place during the week preceding the Holy Spirit day.

The best time for the Holy Spirit day to take place is after the talk on Guidance. However it can happen any time after the talk on Prayer but before the talk on Healing. Make sure it does not clash with any important event. From experience it is important to book the day early and to let relevant authorities, staff, and team members know the dates to avoid last-minute cancellations and claims that "I didn't know about it!"

In some cases it has worked well to give the first talk, "Who Is the Holy Spirit?" at the first session prior to the Holy Spirit day to allow more time on the Holy Spirit day.

Step #7: Order resources and plan follow-up.

The Alpha videos have been used successfully in prisons in the U.K., here in the U.S., and around the world. However, if an experienced speaker can give the Alpha talks using the material from the book, *Questions of Life*, it is often more effective, especially when the speaker has had some experience in prison ministry, or if time is a limitation.

This may also be a better option if the resources are not available in the appropriate language. In some prisons, many of the prisoners do not have a high level of education and may find the Youth Alpha manuals easier to follow. If possible, every prisoner should be provided with an Alpha manual and a Bible. A local church may be able to help provide resources. Some parachurch organizations have been helpful in donating materials to the program as well.

Be sure to obtain permission to bring in and leave your materials.

RESOURCES FOR ALPHA FOR PRISONS

The basic resources needed to run a course for 10 inmates are:
- *Alpha for Prisons Training* manual
- *Questions of Life*
- *Telling Others*
- *Searching Issues*
- *Alpha Team Training* video
- *Alpha Team Training* manual (x4)
- The Alpha Course on video
- Alpha manual (x10)
- Alpha invitations
- Alpha poster pack
- *The God Who Changes Lives*—The story of Paul Cowley video
- Bibles

HOW TO ORDER ALPHA RESOURCES

Alpha U.S. National Office
74 Trinity Place
New York, New York 10006
1-888-WHY-ALPHA (1-888-949-2574)
Fax: 212-406-7521
e-mail: resources@alphausa.org
www.alphausa.org

Alpha Canada National Office
P.O. 153, 3456 Dunbar St.
Vancouver, BC V6S 2C2
Tel: 800-743-0899
Fax: 604-224-6124
e-mail: office@alphacanada.org
www.alphacanada.org*

*Check the Alpha Canada website (Alpha Advisors Page) for downloadable invitations and posters which can be personalized for the prison.

CHAPTER THREE

How to publicize your alpha course

Ninety-nine percent of people attend a course because of a personal invitation from a friend. All other methods of advertising such as posters, newspapers, inserts, and fliers help to raise the level of awareness but are not a substitute. There are a variety of approaches for promoting Alpha for Prisons depending on the set up of the institution itself. You may wish to make use of centralized notice boards. Word of mouth and personal invitations may be more appropriate for men or women staying in the same section of the prison. You will know what is best for your particular prison setting.

NOTE
Remember that any publicity in the prison must have the approval of the relevant officials. It is imperative, therefore, to approach them with your material and get the appropriate signature of approval from them before putting up any posters.

IDEAS FOR RECEPTION

There are many ways to make newcomers feel welcome. Here are a few suggestions.

RECEPTION PACKETS

You may want to have information packets available for newcomers to the prison. This could include:

• Information about chapel services

- An invitation to the next Alpha appetizer and course
- A copy of the booklet *Why Jesus?*
- Any other information which may help them feel more at ease on entering the prison

DISPLAYING ALPHA POSTERS

If security allows, Alpha posters can be placed around the prison. These are an effective way of advertising and will help newcomers to the prison identify how to make contact with you. Posters are left blank so that you can use the space to put contact details, time, and location, etc.

SHOWING THE VIDEO

If time permits you could show *The God Who Changes Lives* video.

ALPHA APPETIZER EVENT

THE EVENT

This could be an event to which you invite prisoners and/or prison officials. The idea is to make it informal and relaxed in order to encourage non-Christians to come and enjoy themselves as well as hear about the Alpha course. It acts as an advertisement for your course. Whatever you decide, make it fun and friendly.

An Alpha Appetizer usually includes the talk, "Christianity: Boring, Untrue, Irrelevant? Specifically, for the prison population, a video is now available called "The God Who Changes Lives," which features HTB Prisons Pastor Paul Cowley's testimony. The video introduces the main points of the talk within a context with which prisoners can identify. It is having a powerful impact on the lives of incarcerated men and women.

Another option has worked for Alpha Prison Advisor Jeff Park. "I have used the Jesus film to get inmates to come out, and at that time explain the Alpha course. The Jesus film always draws a great crowd." A number of volunteers can be invited (about one to every six inmates expected), to lead worship, give testimonies, explain Alpha, and be available for a time of ministry. The appetizer is an excellent way to promote the course to the inmates (very much like the Alpha Supper in the church setting) and gives the chaplain the chance to get an idea of how many inmates will be attending the course.

TESTIMONIES

It may also be a good idea to select one or two people to give a testimony. The best people to do this are those who have found the course of value and whose lives have been changed by God. They need to be brief, sincere, and given by the sort of people that the inmates you are trying to encourage can relate to.

Here are some questions that the host of the appetizer could ask those being interviewed:

- How did you find out about the Alpha course?
- What was the Alpha course like?
- What happened to you in the course?
- What difference has Jesus made in your life?
- What would you say to someone who has not yet taken the course?

PERSONAL INVITATIONS

Alpha courses grow through friends bringing friends. The main way your course will grow is by people who have attended Alpha telling other prisoners about Jesus and inviting them to a subsequent course. The more you run Alpha, the more this builds. Some of those who have just completed a course may ask other prisoners on the next course, but equally they may ask them in a year's time or even in three years' time. This underlines the importance of running Alpha as a rolling program.

One aim of the talk "Why and how should we tell others?" (Talk 12) is to motivate the inmates from your current course to invite other prisoners to the Alpha appetizer and the next Alpha course.

How to run an Alpha course in prison

The structure of the Alpha course in prisons is very close to that used in a church, but will need to be flexible according to which section of the prisoners' day is set aside for the activity. As in baking a cake, the best way to run Alpha is to follow the set recipe. With later courses, there may be adaptations you need to make for a local context. This is acceptable so long as the content of the course is closely followed and that changes are consistent with the copyright statement (see pages 53-54, Appendix G).

A normal Alpha session in a prison usually includes worship, the video or a live talk, and a small group discussion. Although serving a meal may be out of the question, a social time with juice or coffee and cookies is encouraged.

The prisons are a unique and challenging environment. It is important, therefore, to adapt the course in a way that suits both you and the inmates on your course.

POSSIBLE COURSE TIMETABLES

The Alpha Course is a fifteen-session practical introduction to the Christian faith. It is best run over twelve weeks in prison, and ideally, a day should be set aside sometime between the sixth and thirteenth sessions for a Holy Spirit day. This would include the three talks on the Holy Spirit as well as time for worship and ministry. Each other session should last two hours, although this may vary depending on the time allocated by the prison routine.

The following are suggested course timetables, which you may find useful:

THE ALPHA TERM (ONE SESSION PER WEEK, OVER TWELVE WEEKS)

Week 1	(1) The God Who Changes Lives—The story of Paul Cowley video or Christianity: Boring, Untrue, Irrelevant? (Alpha appetizer)
Week 2	(2) Who Is Jesus?
Week 3	(3) Why Did Jesus Die?
Week 4	(4) How Can I Be Sure of My Faith?
Week 5	(5) Why and How Should I Read the Bible?
Week 6	(6) Why and How Do I Pray?
Week 7	(7) How Does God Guide Us?
Holy Spirit Day	(8) Who Is the Holy Spirit?
	(9) What Does the Holy Spirit Do?
	(10) How Can I Be Filled with the Holy Spirit?
Week 8	(11) How Can I Resist Evil?
Week 9	(12) Why and How Should We Tell Others?
Week 10	(13) Does God Heal Today?
Week 11	(14) What about the Church?
Week 12	(15) How Can I Make the Most of the Rest of My Life?

You may be asking, "What about the high turnover of inmates?"—a situation common to many prisons. We feel it is valuable to have the opportunity to sow some seeds in people who are able to do as much of the course as their time in the prison allows.

We would strongly recommend that no newcomers are introduced to the course after week 4. If other people show interest, they should be encouraged to join the next course. It is key that a feeling of group unity, intimacy, trust, and friendship is allowed to develop within the small groups. This cannot happen if new people are joining throughout the course.

It may happen that one group starts with fifteen people, but due to relocation or sentences ending, finishes with four people. Our experience is that one small course which runs well makes more of an impact in the prison than a larger one where groups are constantly having to go back over old ground for the new people joining. There may be inmates relocated from other prisons that have gotten halfway through a course and ask to complete it with you. Again, if possible, encourage them to wait for the next course to start.

FAST-TRACK ALPHA (COMPLETED IN TWO AND A HALF WEEKS)

Some prisons with a high turnover of inmates coming and leaving, such as detention centers have run an intensive ("fast-track") Alpha course over fifteen days, with one session per day. Here follows a suggested timetable for running Alpha in a short period of time.

Week 1

Monday	(1) The God Who Changes Lives—The story of Paul Cowley video or Christianity: Boring, Untrue, Irrelevant? (Alpha appetizer)
Tuesday	(2) Who Is Jesus?
Wednesday	(3) Why Did Jesus Die?
Thursday	(4) How Can I Be Sure of My Faith?
Friday	(5) Why and How Should I Read the Bible?

Week 2

Monday	(6) Why and How Do I Pray?
Tuesday	(7) How Does God Guide Us?
Wednesday	Holy Spirit day
	(8) Who Is the Holy Spirit?
	(9) What Does the Holy Spirit Do?
	(10) How Can I Be Filled with the Holy Spirit?
Thursday	(11) How Can I Resist Evil?
Friday	(12) Why and How Should We Tell Others?

Week 3

Monday	(13) Does God Heal Today?
Tuesday	(14) What about the Church?
Wednesday	(15) How Can I Make the Most of the Rest of My Life?

This is only one of the ways in which Alpha can be condensed into a short period of time. Some prisons run two sessions a day, once a week. Others are able to run the course with two sessions a day over a one and a half week period.

CREATING THE RIGHT ENVIRONMENT FOR ALPHA

• Try not to use a room which is being used for another activity at the same time or which is a thruway to somewhere else. The prison chapel may well

be the best place.
- Have something going on as the inmates arrive. Many courses have music or a music video playing.
- Make it easy for latecomers to join the group without feeling awkward.
- Try not to overrun the session and always finish in good time so as to fit in with the prison routine. Be as flexible as possible. If you have time remaining after the discussion groups you may like to have a time for relaxed fellowship and getting to know each other. This is a great way to form friendships and encourage people to come back each week.
- Refer to prisoners attending the Alpha course as "guests."

FOOD AND ALPHA

Food has always been an important part of the Alpha course. It makes inmates feel special and valuable. It provides the setting in which people get to know each other and form lasting friendships. Experience has shown that courses that have run without a meal find that there is not as much fellowship in the small groups. The coffee or juice and cookies served at the Alpha course should be a bit different from normal prison life. If allowed, home baked cakes or cookies could be provided. The meal time also enables leaders and helpers to get to know the inmates in a more relaxed environment without discussing any spiritual issues but simply finding out how the past week has gone.

One Prison Advisor states, "Often we bring in large, sealed bags of popcorn and soft drinks or bagged chips. This works well for videos. Negotiating for a full meal for the Celebration Dinner is also important. Most authorities will allow a pizza party when the pizza is delivered directly to the prison."

WORSHIP AND ALPHA

Depending on the setting, it is best to try and have some form of worship. We have found that although many find the singing the most difficult part of the course to begin with, it is often the part they enjoy most by the end of the course. For many people, their first experience of communicating with God takes place during a hymn or spiritual song. It also helps people to make the step from Alpha in prison to church, where the worship of God is central. You might want to look at the song books available in the prison and see if they need updating with some modern Christian songs.

Unless worship can be led and music played competently, it is probably best not done at all. Smaller courses (10 people or less) may feel conspicuous singing out loud. Perhaps you could begin the evening with a vocalist singing two to three worship songs or listen to a couple of worship songs on CD. This method introduces the group to worship but doesn't demand participation. Where this idea has been used, inmates have commented on how much they enjoyed the music.

If you would like more information about worship, look at the *Alpha Worship Pack* (with cassette or CD). This is a comprehensive training resource for those wishing to introduce worship to the Alpha course. It is specifically designed for Alpha course leaders, worship leaders, and music teams but is also suitable for use within smaller groups for unaccompanied worship.

Following are some useful tips you may wish to pass on to the worship leader on your course.

PREPARATION

It is very useful to have attended a good worship leading course. It is also good to have done one or two visits with a more experienced worship leader.

Keep it simple, but try to have available:

- full set of overhead transparencies
- blank transparency sheets and pens
- amplifier, worship tape, and cassette player
- 20–30 songbooks (in case there is no overhead projector)

RESEARCH

Find out the nature of the institution (young offenders, male/female prison, high or low security prison, etc.) Learn the rules and regulations for volunteers at that institution.

SONG SELECTION

This is very much a personal choice and also depends upon the songs you know and are comfortable playing. Below is a list of some of the songs that have been well received in some courses. Remember also to be open to the prompting of the Holy Spirit on which songs to use.

Hymns such as:	
	Amazing Grace
	There Is a Redeemer
	Be Thou My Vision
	When I Survey the Wondrous Cross
	The Old Rugged Cross

Other songs:	
	Come Now Is the Time to Worship
	Salvation Belongs to our God
	By His Grace
	Open the Eyes of my Heart
	Overwhelmed by Love
	Lord I Lift Your Name on High
	Faithful One

Action songs:	
	Blessed Be the Name of the Lord
	Jesus I Love You Deep Down in my Heart

If there is enough time prior to the visit, it can help to ask the chaplain for a list of the songs that are familiar to the inmates, or are their particular favorites, so that some of these can be included. Do not, however, be hindered from teaching them one or two new songs as this can be quite refreshing.

DURING THE WORSHIP TIME

Be assertive. Saying, "Let's stand to worship God" helps people know you are in charge. Start with confidence and the men or women will follow your lead. Try to avoid speaking between songs to keep the flow of worship.

PRAYER

Establish a prayer team to pray for the team, the chaplain, and the guests. Have people praying for you before you go and during the visit. You may feel spiritually "deflated" following the visit so make sure you have someone to pray with afterward.

FEEDBACK

As the course leader you may like to ask the worship leader to provide you with some feedback from the worship. Here are some questions you may like to include on your feedback form:

- What songs did you use?
- What equipment was available?
- Were there any musically gifted prisoners who were able to help you?

If in doubt about anything do not be afraid to ask the Alpha North America Office Alpha Prison Advisors, or other worship leaders who have done prison visits.

PRAYER AND ALPHA

"Evangelism without prayer is like a bomb without a detonator and prayer without evangelism is like a detonator without a bomb."
(Dutch Sheets, The Prayer Summit)

In other words, we need both prayer and evangelism to be effective.

The main aim of the Alpha course is to bring the good news of Jesus Christ to those who don't know Him. This work can only be done when it is covered in prayer, and we strongly suggest that, in addition to praying regularly with your team, you form a prayer group to support you. Holy Trinity Brompton in London has formulated an Adopt-a-Prison plan for its home groups, where the group adopts a particular prison to pray for the Alpha course running there, for the chaplaincy and volunteer teams, and for the prisoners. This is a format that other churches could adopt and use.

It is invaluable to meet together as a team to pray before and after each session. This will not only benefit the inmates but will also have the very positive effect of bonding the team together more closely.

As a group leader, you may like to pray for the people coming into your group. Pray that they would mix well and that good friendships would form. Once you have met the group, we would encourage you to pray for them daily in your own time. Opportunities for prayer with the inmates come especially on the Holy Spirit day and after the Healing talk. Make sure the team is prepared for this.

For more information on prayer you may like to listen to the *Prayer on Alpha* seminar which is now available on video or audio cassette.

Giving a Short Testimony

It is always possible to argue over facts. A personal testimony, however, can make the same point via a different route. We are all intrigued by the way other people choose to live their lives. People will be fascinated by the insights into your life. For an even greater impact, interview one of the prisoners. An interview is less daunting than a monologue, and it enables you to shape the content of what they say. The content of the testimony should be either, "How I came to Christ" or "What Jesus means to me today".

- Testimonies should be brief, honest, and give God the glory rather than your former lifestyle.
- Don't preach. Avoid church jargon.
- Try to include biblical truths.

Suggested video clips and creative illustrations

Many young offender institutions and some adult prisons use video clips as part of their talks. These are useful for raising questions, setting up an issue or illustrating a point in a dramatic, visual way.

DON'T

- explain the content of the clip—this will weaken the impact
- use video clips just as a gimmick

DO

- check the film well in advance—sometimes a clip isn't as you remember it
- make sure someone present has full mastery of the technology before you use it

Think through how you will introduce the clip and how you will follow it up immediately afterward.

WHO IS JESUS?

Forrest Gump. He runs across America "for no particular reason." He builds up a large following of people and then suddenly stops and makes his way home. Make the point that all of us follow something or someone: pop stars, fashion icons, sports heroes... Do we know why we are following them?

WHY DID JESUS DIE?

The Mission. The scene where Robert De Niro has a huge weight of armor cut away by the natives he used to hunt. (Make the point that this is a powerful display of forgiveness and the price had been paid.)

Indiana Jones and the Last Crusade. Final dramatic scene: penitent men bow before the breath of God; walk in the steps of God; take a step of faith. Make the point that we have to take that step of faith.

Armageddon. Bruce Willis dies to save the world so that his daughter can have love. Makes the point that Jesus sacrificed His life so that we can love God.

HOW CAN I BE SURE OF MY FAITH?

Lay out several glasses of different types of Cola (one being *Coca Cola*), making sure all labels are hidden. Ask the group to sample the drinks and see if they can identify the *Coca Cola*—"the real thing." Make the point that in order to discover "the real thing" for themselves, they actually had to sample it. And so it is with Christianity.

HOW AND WHY SHOULD I READ MY BIBLE?

The Simpsons. When Homer refuses to go to church and God comes down and talks to him and encourages him to do what he likes. Make the point that the Bible is God's manual for life and the main way in which God reveals Himself to us.

The Gospel of Matthew and the Book of Acts are now available on video. Both scripts follow the N.I.V. word for word. Various clips can be used to bring the Bible to life.

WHY AND HOW DO I PRAY?

Video TV News. Play this to the group and then invite short prayers relating to the areas covered.

Find any clip from a film with a child talking to a father. Go on to explain that prayer is like the communication between a father and a child. Put this into practice by allowing inmates to pray for each other.

HOW DOES GOD GUIDE US?

Illustration. Ships and other sea vessels often use two or three fixed points on shore (such as a house, a tree, and a telegraph pole) in order to ascertain or maintain their exact position. Make the point that we can often feel "all at sea" but that God provides various ways for us to know where we stand with Him.

HOW CAN I BE FILLED WITH THE HOLY SPIRIT?

Balloon. Partially fill a balloon with air; this can be likened to a person having the Holy Spirit. Continue and fill the balloon more and more; this is like being filled with the Holy Spirit. Release the balloon and you can illustrate how we can leak and therefore need constant filling.

Bring in a soft football and have it tossed around the room. Then fill it up with a hand pump and toss it around again to illustrate how we "leak" spiritually and need filling.

HOW CAN I RESIST EVIL?

Return of the Jedi. Use the scene where Luke Skywalker fights Darth Vader to illustrate how to resist evil.

Chariots of Fire. It's not when you fall that you fail—get up!

The Matrix. The fight scene toward the end when Neo is fighting the agents, is a good example of resisting evil.

WHY AND HOW SHOULD WE TELL OTHERS?

Light of the World. Give each member of the group a candle. Try to make the room as dark as possible and then light a candle. Use this candle to light the candle of people on either side of you. They in turn light their neighbors' candles and so on until the whole group have their candles lit. Make the point that the whole group can be "lit" simply by everyone "lighting" their neighbor. Note: Some prisons have "no smoking" so matches may be banned.

DOES GOD HEAL TODAY?

The Matrix. The scene when Neo dies and is brought back to life by Trinity's loving words.

WHAT ABOUT THE CHURCH?

Sister Act. Find an appropriate scene, such as the scene where the nuns set up a recreation area for the young people in the community, to show the importance of church.

Mr Bean in Church. Funny example of church life.

HOW CAN I MAKE THE MOST OF THE REST OF MY LIFE?

Dead Poets Society. Use the "seize the day" clip to highlight the importance of making the most of life.

Back to the Future. Choose clips which show how the decisions we make affect our lives in the future.

Groundhog Day. Clips to show that each day we are responsible for the right/wrong choices or decisions that we make.

Saving Private Ryan. At the end Private Ryan asks his wife to tell him he has been a good man and lived a life worthy of all those who sacrificed their lives to save him. This makes the point that we are not good and have not lived a worthy life unless it is lived wholeheartedly and committed to Christ —Romans 12:1.

Copyright: The law is confusing over the use of specific video clips as suggested in this manual. Film and video companies have advised that technically it is illegal to show all or part of a rented film to anyone other than your family. However, in practice the law is extremely difficult to interpret. Normally distribution companies do not mind clips of their films being shown as long as:

- it is only a tiny part of the whole film
- no money is changing hands
- no profit is being made

AT THE END OF THE COURSE

As inmates receive certificates for many of the educational courses completed in prison, you may wish to issue the participants an Alpha certificate. This shows that they have completed all or most of the course and provides something to discuss with family and friends. (We have found some instances where a family member is also taking an Alpha course on the outside.) Many of the inmates like to display the certificates in their cells. It is also useful when attending a church after being released, to show that they have completed an Alpha course (see Appendix C, page 44).

Some teams issue beautifully prepared certificates and at the presentation allow each participant to talk about what he or she experienced during the course. When this is done during the Celebration Dinner, each inmate can invite an inmate guest, forming the foundation for the next course. It is also helpful to receive feedback from the course in order to improve each time on things that could have been done better. For this we use two different feedback forms. One is for each of the inmates who have done the course, and the other is for the team from local churches who have been involved in leading and helping (see Appendix D, pages 45-48).

CHAPTER FIVE

THE HOLY SPIRIT DAY

The Holy Spirit day in the prison has the same aim as the Holy Spirit weekend in the church context, which is to teach about the Holy Spirit and provide individual ministry for the inmates. The teaching on the person and work of the Holy Spirit is a vital part of the course and should not be missed.

Instead of the regular morning, afternoon, or evening group it's best to put in a special request to the relevant authority to secure a day with the inmates, set aside for this purpose. If possible, the whole group should be allowed to eat lunch together. This has been found to be a powerful and effective time, which has a profound effect on the lives of those on the course.

It is important that your team is equipped and experienced in ministering in the Holy Spirit. Often, a team from a church outside the prison can be invited to run the day, especially if you are short of leaders and helpers in your small groups.

GENERAL INFORMATION

TIMING

The ideal time for the Holy Spirit day is between the talks on "Guidance" and "Resisting Evil." It should always fall between the talks on "Prayer" and "Healing." It is always preferable to have the talk "How Can I Resist Evil?" following the weekend. If necessary switch around the talks on evil and guidance.

LOCATIONS

You may like to have a change of scenery from your usual meeting place. If possible, you could try to book another room in the prison. The chapel is most often the ideal place for the day, but sometimes lunch can be arranged in another room.

FOOD

We have found the lunch time on the Holy Spirit day to be a really special time of fellowship when inmates and team can get to know each other better. This is encouraging for both inmates and team, and those who have managed to have a meal together on the day have said that the entire atmosphere of the day was really positive.

Both high and low security prisons have been able to do this. Ask the relevant official for permission for this special one-time occasion. You might have the prison kitchen deliver the food to the chapel to eat during the course of the Holy Spirit day.

In one prison where the inmates were not allowed to share a meal together due to the high security level of the prison, the chaplain continued with his request persistently before each course. They are now able to share the meal together although this was only allowed after having run the course for two years. Some of the men on that course commented that they had not shared a meal with anybody for nine years.

PRAYER MINISTRY

Plan in advance how you will handle the ministry time as some set-up, moving of chairs, or another room may be required.

INVITING GUEST SPEAKERS

If you would like someone to lead your Holy Spirit day, we suggest working with your local church for ideas about speakers. Or contact Alpha North America to see if there is anyone in your state who has run Alpha and would like to help with the talks. Live speakers are recommended for the day even if you have been using videos for the rest of the course.

SUGGESTED TIMETABLE

A suggested timetable showing how the day could be structured is set out below. This could be altered according to the time frame of the specific prison. Videos can be used for the day, or talks can be given, or a combination of both, and worship, testimony, and a time of ministry are all important aspects of the day.

8:30 a.m.	Arrive at the prison gates/meet up with rest of team
9:00 a.m.	Set-up, team-briefing & prayer
9:30 a.m.	Greet the inmates
9:40 a.m.	Introduce the team & worship
10:00 a.m.	Talk: Who Is the Holy Spirit?
10:35 a.m.	Coffee break
10:50 a.m.	Talk: What Does the Holy Spirit Do? (Follow the talk with a brief meditation time so participants may respond to the prompting of the Holy Spirit.)
11:30 a.m.	Lunch
1:30 p.m.	Discussion groups
2:15 p.m.	Talk: How Can I Be Filled with the Holy Spirit?
4:00 p.m.	Worship & ministry
4:45 p.m.	Coffee/juice
5:15 p.m.	Close & depart

CHECKLIST

It may be worth noting the following as a reminder of what to tell the inmates to bring with them. It is always a good idea to brings spares of everything just in case items are forgotten!

Don't forget to bring:
• Bible
• Alpha manual
• Notebook & pencil

Make sure <u>all</u> items brought in for the day are taken out.

CHAPTER SIX

FOLLOWING ALPHA

It is so important that inmates who become Christians in Alpha are nurtured and supported after the course. They should be encouraged to join regular chapel activities and services, and should be a part of a small Bible study group if at all possible. There are several resources for use after Alpha which are all available from Alpha North America or Alpha Canada (see page 15 for contact information).

EXPECT FRUIT AND PLAN

Conversion may take place in a moment, but it is part of a process. Jesus used the expression "born again" (John 3:3) for the beginning of a spiritual life, and the New Testament speaks about becoming a child of God. While the birth of a child occurs on one day (usually!), there is a much longer process before and after.

New Christians need to be integrated into the life of the Christian community, and appropriate ways of doing this will vary. If you are running Alpha on a regular basis in your prison, follow up will be obvious. But for those who may be leaving the prison at the end of your course, it is important to plan ahead and decide how you will encourage new Christians. You may like to make contact with the prison where they are being transferred to or a church where they will worship on release to see what follow-up is available for them.

On release inmates should be encouraged to join a church community in their area, which would be prepared to help them in practical ways such as finding clothing, accommodation, and employment, as well as to nurture them in their faith.

FOLLOW-UP RESOURCES

A number of resources have been compiled with the aim being to give people solid biblical roots for their faith and lifestyle, and to address problems and difficult issues in a clear and simple way. These include:

A LIFE WORTH LIVING

A nine-week course based on the Book of Philippians. The material has been written specifically for those who are just starting out in the Christian life. The manual can be used with the book, audio cassette, or videos.

SEARCHING ISSUES

This tackles the seven issues most often raised in Alpha such as the question of suffering, the validity of other religions, or sex before marriage. The manual can be used with the book or audio cassette.

CHALLENGING LIFESTYLE

Nineteen Bible studies which seek to apply Jesus' teaching on the Sermon on the Mount to the details of our daily lives. This material aims to inspire and encourage new believers as they seek to live out their faith. The manual can be used with the book or audio cassette.

THE HEART OF REVIVAL

Ten Bible studies based on the Book of Isaiah, drawing out important truths for today by interpreting some of the teaching of the Old Testament Prophet Isaiah. The book seeks to understand what revival might mean and how we can prepare to be part of it. The manual can be used with the book or audio cassette.

If you would like to order any of these resources or any other Alpha resources you can obtain them from your local stockist or by calling Alpha North America or Alpha Canada (see page 15).

CARING FOR EX-OFFENDERS – THE LOCAL CHURCH

FOLLOW-UP AFTER RELEASE

We pray that all Alpha graduates will want to continue in their Christian faith, and so it is good to encourage them to think about what they will do in terms of church when they are released from prison.

Wherever possible, links should be built up before they are released with a church in the area where the inmate is going to live. It is possible that they may already have a church link, and if so, this should be encouraged, so that they feel they have a community of God's people to which they belong outside prison.

It is important to work with whatever group or individual is involved with discharge planning (re-settlement) at the prison and ensure that the Alpha graduate is met at the prison gate and provided with the support required.

WORKING WITH THE CHURCH

If the prison is a local one, and the inmate is planning to settle near to the prison after release, then any links already formed with churches in the area, would be good to pursue.

If the inmate is moving away from the immediate area of the prison, then a church will need to be found in the area where he or she will be living. The Alpha Register can assist in this search.

CHAPTER SEVEN

TO CONCLUDE

Alpha contains the truth of the Gospel. Be encouraged as you prepare, teach, and lead each session. Be prayerful and committed to the men or women you come across. Then they will know the truth, and the truth will set them free (John 8:32).

We hope that this manual has shown you how Alpha can be used in prison as an effective tool of evangelism to reach out to the prisoners you work with. We have found that time and again God has honored simple requests for Him to send His Spirit among us. Amazing and profound changes always occur as a result. We continue to see men and women giving their lives to Christ, being filled with the Spirit, and getting excited about Jesus. We hope that you will find Alpha an easy way to present the Christian message in a nonthreatening manner which is relevant to men and women in prison today.

APPENDIX A

COMMON QUESTIONS AND ANSWERS ABOUT ALPHA FOR PRISONS

WOULD YOU RECOMMEND DOING THE ALPHA COURSE WITH VIDEOS OR WITH LIVE SPEAKERS?

We recognize that the ideal in the end is to have live speakers but we recommend that people start their courses with the videos for three reasons:

1. To prepare 15 talks in a term and to prepare them really well is extremely hard work.
2. If it is your first Alpha course, there are a lot of things to organize apart from the talks.
3. If the course is small, it is an advantage to watch the talk on video. This makes the discussion easier as the speaker is not also the group leader and the expression of contrary opinion is less threatening.

Here are three alternate ways of running your course:

- Stop the video halfway at a logical point for a coffee break before finishing off the video (45 minutes is a long time to concentrate!)
- Start talk on video and break at a logical point. Continue with a live speaker after a coffee break
- Start with a speaker and finish off with a section from the video

If you find one talk too long for a session you can break the talk at an appropriate moment and continue with the rest the following week.

WHAT ABOUT DOING TWO TALKS IN A WEEK/NIGHT?

The whole feel of Alpha is process evangelism. It is about walking with people and what happens between sessions is just as important as what happens at Alpha. So if possible try not to merge the talks unless you feel it is right for your group.

HOW DO YOU ENCOURAGE INMATES NOT TO DROP OUT?

The best thing you can do is to be really organized, to plan the course, and to set the dates and provide a printed schedule. This will help inmates know what the course involves and to fit it into their schedule.

IN THE SMALL GROUP, DO YOU MAINLY HAVE A DISCUSSION OR STUDY THE BIBLE?

We encourage guests to ask questions, make comments and observations, discuss and debate with each other. When or if the leader feels it is appropriate, it may then be possible to move on to Bible study. In some prisons a Bible study is held on a separate evening.

WHAT DO YOU DO IF ONE PERSON DOMINATES THE GROUP?

Here skill is required from the leader of the small group to draw out answers from other people and to include the whole group in the discussion (see *Telling Others,* chapter 7). You may want to try sitting beside the dominating person.

WHAT DO YOU DO IF NO ONE IN THE GROUP WILL SAY ANYTHING?

Two questions that normally get people talking in a group are:
• What did anyone think of the talk?
• What does anyone feel about the talk?

Following that, refer to the discussion questions in the *Alpha Team Training* manual or Leader's Guide. Do not be anxious if people are quiet for a little bit after you have asked them a question. Often it takes people time to think through what they want to say. Some groups have made a list of questions on the first session for easy reference.

WHAT HAPPENS IF SOMEONE IN MY SMALL GROUP HAS GOT A REALLY SERIOUS PROBLEM?

Each Alpha course should have a pastoral care structure in place whereby each inmate is looked after by a leader or helper and each leader or helper is looked after by the prison chaplain. As problems arise, they can go up this structure of pastoral care to the appropriate level.

MUST PEOPLE ATTEND EVERY SESSION?

We ask those helping or leading the course to be 100 percent committed to it and to come every week and to the Holy Spirit day. However, it is the opposite for those who are inmates on the course: they may come and go as they wish (see *Telling Others,* chapter 3).

APPENDIX B

WHAT PEOPLE ARE SAYING ABOUT ALPHA FOR PRISONS

"I know of many people whose lives have been transformed through the Alpha course. I rejoice how God is using it so powerfully to renew many churches both inside and outside prison walls."
Chuck Colson, Founder, Prison Fellowship Ministries

"I have prayerfully and carefully examined the Alpha curriculum and found it to be a powerful evangelism tool to turn people from crime to Christ. Alpha offers those caught in the criminal justice system web a solution to the question of safety, quality of life, transformation, healing, restoration, and prosperity that can be passed on to future generations. The Alpha courses that are running in the Texas Dept. of Criminal Justice are providing renewed hope to inmates and officers alike and works to build a safer state and nation for all our citizens."
Jerry Groom, Head Chaplain, Texas Dept. of Prisons

"Alpha provides a strong foundation of faith for new believers in the jail and prison. By going through Alpha, we are able to build a true friendship with the men where they see Christ in us and we in them so they desire a continuum of care and discipleship even beyond incarceration to our aftercare center and church."
Senior Chaplain, York County Detention Center, Associate Pastor of Forest Hill Church, Charlotte, North Carolina

"Newly released from prison, alcohol and drug free, I felt the pull of the old life, and didn't want to go there. A lady I knew invited me to Alpha at her church. I went because I had nothing to lose. I met Jesus the first night, and he has transformed my life. That was nearly six years ago and I now help with an Alpha Course in prison, and am truly blessed. Alpha is the best thing since sliced bread."
Shelly, Ontario, Canada

"There is such a balance of grace and truth in the Alpha teaching. I needed to receive that grace so I could love God and myself. Now for the first time, I am hungry to learn more about God."
Cleetus C., Charlotte Correction Center, Charlotte, NC

"God used this Alpha course change my life, not by any super revelation of new teaching, but by reaffirming the Bible truths and allowing us to discuss them together. I really know now what I believe and find myself sharing it with others like never before."
Kevin H., Charlotte Correction Center, Charlotte, NC

"I learned from Alpha that being a Christian can be fun. This was apparent each time our group would meet. I've made the commitment to start over in Christ. I've died in my old ways and I'm being resurrected in Christ in my new life. The mistakes I've made are over with and I've asked God to forgive me, and now I'm able to forgive myself."
Sherri, Halbert State Prison, Texas, U.S.A

"The inmates attending Alpha courses are very appreciative of the fact that they are cared for spiritually and also that they can have a personal relationship with our Lord and Savior. We have seen tremendous changes in their attitudes and their relationship with their fellow inmates and the guards. Nicky Gumbel is presenting the gospel in a way to them that they can understand and grasp, what Jesus Christ can and is doing in their lives."
Mr. & Mrs. Josef Roswitha
Alpha in Prison Leaders, Cheshire Correctional Institute, Cheshire, CT

The following pages include forms designed to be enlarged, photocopied, and used on your Alpha course:

Appendix C:

Certificate

Appendix D:

Feedback forms
- Course feedback form—for inmates to fill in on completion of the course
- Team feedback form—for course leaders and helpers to fill in at the end of the course

Appendix E:

Visitor's information sheet

Alpha North America

"Do not let the world squeeze you into its mold... Let God remold you from within... then you will know God's good and perfect will."

Romans 12:1-2

This Certificate Is Awarded

to

_____

on completion of

The Alpha Course

_____

Date: _____

Signature: _____

Topic areas covered:

Who is Jesus?
Why did Jesus die?
How can I be sure of my faith?
Why and how should I read the Bible?
Why and how do I pray?

Who is the Holy Spirit?
What does the Holy Spirit do?
How can I be filled with the Spirit?
How can I resist evil?
How does God Guide us?

Why and how should we tell others?
Does God heal today?
What about the church?
How can I make the most of the rest of my life?

COURSE FEEDBACK FORM

Name/Number: _____

Prison: _____

Date of course: _____

Chaplain's name: _____

How did you hear about the Alpha course? _____

_____

Why did you decide to do Alpha? _____

_____

How many sessions did you attend? _____

Were you a regular chapelgoer when you started the course? _____

_____

Were you a Christian when you started the course? _____

How would you describe yourself now (in terms of the Christian faith)? _____

_____

If the answers to the previous two questions are different, when and how did the change occur? _____

_____

_____

In what ways, if any, did you benefit from doing the Alpha course? _____

_____

_____

What did you enjoy most? _____

_____

What did you find most difficult?

_____

_____

In what way could the course be improved for use in Prisons?

_____

Talks

_____

_____

_____

Small groups

_____

_____

_____

Generally

_____

_____

_____

Would you be interested in being discipled by a church in your home area once you are released?

_____

_____

If so, what is your release date/where will you be released to:

_____

_____

Team Feedback Form

Name:

Dates of course:

How might you have changed the program to make the course even more effective?

Please write below
Any prophetic words or pictures/ thoughts you might have had during and following the course.

Experiences that were significant to you during the course.

Administration
What other information could we have given you that would have been helpful prior to helping on the course?

Future visits
Would you be available to help on future courses?

_____

_____

_____

Follow up
Were there any prisoners you spoke with or prayed for who would benefit
from follow up by the chaplaincy team? We are especially eager to help
men and women who are leaving in the near future and need support.

_____

_____

_____

_____

Please add any other comments

_____

_____

_____

_____

_____

_____

_____

_____

_____

VISITORS' INFORMATION SHEET

1. Prison volunteers can only come to the prison (chapel) at the invitation of the chaplain.

2. Prior arrangements must be made and names submitted. These may be subject to security checking. For some prisons, this needs to be done at least a month before the visit.

3. Children under the age of eighteen will not usually be allowed into the prison.

4. Visitors should ALWAYS bring personal identification, i.e., passport, photo i.d. or drivers license and report at the gate when arriving.

5. It is advisable to bring only the minimum of valuables into the prison.

6. Mobile phones and cameras MUST NOT be brought in.

7. Alcohol MUST NOT be brought in.

8. Drugs MUST NOT be brought in (prescription drugs should be left in your car if not required).

9. Please ensure that wallets, purses, etc. are locked in the Chaplain's office before the meeting.

10. You are likely to be searched on arrival.

11. You will always be escorted through the prison.

12. Male visitors may be required to have their image recorded on video.

13. Always listen to advice and direction from prison staff and act on it.

14. You are not permitted to hand ANYTHING to a prisoner. It is an offense which can carry a heavy prison sentence.

15. You are not permitted to receive ANYTHING from a prisoner.

16. You must not give personal details to a prisoner.

17. Personal correspondence is not encouraged. If letters are written they must be via an official body when written to you.

18. Please do not offer or agree to carry messages, either "in" or "out", either

written or verbal, from one prison to another or from one person to another.

19. Instructions given by any member of staff must be followed without question.

20. Be careful while in conversation or while giving talks to use appropriate terms at all times.

21. If officers are present during meetings do not attempt to involve them unless they clearly wish it.

22. In the unlikely event of trouble during your visit do not get involved in any way. Follow instructions given at the time.

23. Please be modest in dress (no short skirts or tight trousers),no aftershave/perfume. Prisoners can get the wrong idea.

24. If you are approached by a prisoner seeking information or making requests that cause you the slightest concern inform a member of staff. If you know the name of the prisoner it is always helpful!

25. Remember prisoners have everything to gain from their contact and relationship with you. You may have everything to lose.

26. Never let yourself be put in a position of compromise. You may think this could not happen to you but IT CAN. Some prisoners are extremely skilled in conversation and relationships. They can easily find your weak spot.

27. Please don't make promises to prisoners that you cannot keep.

28. Always respect staff. You may not always understand their actions and even feel critical of them at times. Remember they have a difficult job and often have an awareness that you will not have.

29. Remember at all times you are in a prison.

30. Be alert and observant.

31. If in doubt—ASK!

32. Having said all this enjoy your visit because prisoners are people and will certainly appreciate the time and consideration you have given them.

*If you have any doubts regarding security contact the prison chaplain.

Appendix F

ALPHA FOR PRISONS QUESTIONNAIRE

To help assess the effectiveness of the Alpha course in prison, we would appreciate it if you could please copy, complete, and send to Alpha North America, 74 Trinity Place, New York, NY 10006. In Canada, send to: Alpha Canada, 3456 Dunbar St., Vancouver, B.C., V6S 2C2.

Chaplain or Alpha group leader's title & name:
_____

Prison:
_____

When did you run your first Alpha course in prison:
_____

_____

Did you use: Videos?   Speakers?
_____

Who ran the course? (e.g. Chaplain or volunteers)
_____

In which part of the day did you run the course?
_____

How much time were you allowed for a session?
_____

How many attended the course?
_____

Did you split into groups for discussion?
_____

Did inmates lead the discussion groups?
_____

Did you involve local churches in running your Holy Spirit day (in addition to your regular volunteer team)?
_____

Did you have any problems or difficulties running Alpha?
_____

_____

_____

_____

_____

_____

Any other comments:

_____

_____

_____

_____

_____

_____

_____

Appendix G

ALPHA COPYRIGHT STATEMENT

Sandy Millar, Vicar of Holy Trinity Brompton, writes:

"We have always been keen to allow individuals who are running an Alpha course the flexibility to adapt where it was felt necessary to allow for locally felt needs and where there was the desire to retain the essential elements, nature, and identity of the course. Experience has shown though that this has been misunderstood and the resulting loss of integrity in some courses has given rise to considerable confusion. Now that Alpha is running all around the world we have reluctantly had to draw up a copyright statement more tightly in order to preserve confidence and quality control. I am sure you will understand."

(1) With the exception of books published by Kingsway (in which the author is stated to hold the copyright), all Alpha resources and materials, including graphics materials, booklets, and tapes are copyright to Holy Trinity Brompton.

(2) In no circumstances may any part of any Alpha resource be reproduced or transmitted in any form or by any means, electronic or mechanical, including photocopying, recording, or any information storage or retrieval system, without permission in writing from the copyright holder or that holder's agent.

(3) Use of Alpha resources is permitted only when in conjunction with the running or promotion of an Alpha course. Resale, or the obtaining of payment in any other connection with any Alpha resource is not permitted.

(4) Holy Trinity Brompton asks that the name "Alpha," or names similar to it should not be used in connection with any other Christian course. This request is made in order to:

- avoid confusion caused by different courses having similar titles;
- ensure the uniformity and integrity of the Alpha course; and
- to maintain confidence in courses listed on the Alpha register.

(5) Holy Trinity Brompton accepts that minor adaptations to the Alpha course may occasionally be desirable. These should only concern the length of the talks or the number of sessions. In each case the essential character of the course must be retained. Alpha is a series of 15 talks, given over a period of time, including a weekend or day away, with teaching based on all the material in *Questions of Life*. If the Alpha course is adapted, the person responsible must:

- only use such a course in their own church or parish;
- not allow such a course to be used elsewhere; and
- not publish or promote such a course.

This statement supersedes all previous statements relating to copyright in any Alpha resource.

NOTES

NOTES